Every Journey
Starts With a
Single Step...

Write . Draw . Imagine

Take a look at your life now and explore in detail what might be holding you back; face your greatest nemesis and realise your true potential.

Challenge yourself to be better in this integrative process that walks you through the stages of growth and expansion.

You are the creator of your own life experience – so start creating.

Includes additional exercises that invite you to go within and feel for the answers.

Written and Produced by TLC

STEP 1

>>>>>>>>>>

My Life Right Now

- How do you feel about your life right now?
- What does it look like?

Taking a candid look at our world can help identify areas where we might be missing something, or not living life to its full potential. And we can get so caught up in our every day that we forget what it is we actually want and what we came here to do. Are we really enjoying our lives and embracing the full experience of our time here on earth? Focus on what your life looks like to you; it doesn't have to be literal. It can be a representation – colour, shape, form.

 *Not sure?* See next page for Tips.

WRITE

Describe how your life looks and feels to you right now.

_____

_____

_____

_____

_____

_____

_____

_____

_____

_____

_____

_____

_____

_____

_____

_____

_____

_____

_____

_____

_____

Tips

- Perhaps you're a mum or dad and your world looks like washing and preparing endless meals.
- Maybe you have a full time job and your world revolves around that.
- You could have no money and be living on the streets.
- You could have everything you've ever wanted but are still unsatisfied.
- You don't really do much but you don't really aspire to do anything anyway.
- You're depressed and can barely get up in the morning.
- You know there must be more to life than this.

Perhaps your life looks ok, nothing to complain about really. It's certainly better than some people's. And what choice do you really have anyway? Life is what it is, right? Actually, no. We always have a choice. We are the creators of our life experience; everything in our external environment is a reflection of our internal environment. Don't like something in our life? We have the power to change it.

Still Not Sure?

Let's do a little exercise that might help:
It's called  'Feel Inside for What's Trying to Hide'

Close your eyes, take a few slow, deep belly breaths. Focus on your life as it is now. Notice how it feels in the body – is there a sensation; perhaps a feeling of panic, apathy, or even regret? Notice whereabouts the feeling is in the body; it could be in your heart, your gut, your neck. Let your mind take you there. Breathe slowly through that area. Be present with it. It's just showing you where your energy isn't flowing in the way it should.

Now see how you feel about your life. Has the feeling changed?
What does it look like? Draw or write about it in your journal.

DRAW

If you could draw a representation of your world right now, what would it be like?

STEP 2

>>>>>>>>>

A Sign

- Is there something you would rather be doing?
- What keeps calling to you?
- Where does your passion lie?

Is there something that you always put to the bottom of the pile; tell yourself you'll get to it when you've done all the other jobs? Is it perhaps something you'd rather be doing but don't know when you'll have time or even the inclination? Now is your chance to expose that cheeky little desire, shine a light on it. It's pestering you for a reason.

Not sure? See next page for Tips.

WRITE

Explore what's missing from your life as it is now, and how it could be different.

_____

_____

_____

_____

_____

_____

_____

_____

_____

_____

_____

_____

_____

_____

_____

_____

_____

_____

_____

_____

_____

_____

Tips

- Perhaps you would rather be a writer, you've always enjoyed writing ever since you were little.
- You love helping people, you're such a good listener, you're great at advice.
- You love watching birds fly, you wish you could fly, you've always wanted to learn to be a pilot.
- You love cooking, it gives you pleasure to create dishes for others to enjoy.
- You always have good ideas for how to make things work better, you're an inventor at heart.
- Perhaps you love playing with children, they inspire you.
- Being out in nature is your favourite thing.

Can't think of anything specific? That's ok, things will become clearer as we go along, it's all part of this wonderful journey of discovery. In the meantime, think of something you enjoy. What lights you up? What fills your cup? What did you enjoy as a child? Sometimes it's just an awareness that there is more to life than the drudgery of every day. Here is where you start from.

Still Not Sure?

Let's do a little exercise that might help:
It's called **'Feel the Feeling you Don't want to Feel'**

Close your eyes, take a few slow, deep belly breaths. Focus on the question: What would I rather be doing? Notice how it feels in the body – there'll be a sensation, like a knot or an ache, or maybe panic. Notice where the sensation is located and imagine that it's a discontented baby or puppy that needs soothing. It won't stay still, it's writhing around making you feel uncomfortable. But stick with it. Perhaps put your hand on the place, imagine calming the baby or puppy, stroking it, hugging it, loving it, until it starts to calm down. Breathe through the area as if the breath is doing the soothing. After a while, you will notice the sensation start to dissipate and subside.

Now see how you feel about the thing that you would rather be doing. Has the feeling changed? Draw or write about it in your journal.

DRAW

If you could draw a representation of what you would rather be doing, what would it be?

STEP 3

>>>>>>>>>>>

Doubt and Denial

- What's holding you back from doing the thing you most want to do?
- What story are you telling yourself and others?

There is often an excuse or story we tell ourselves and others about why we aren't doing the thing we most want to do. It can be anything from not enough time, to someone else is stopping me, or perhaps, I can't afford it. It often comes with a lengthy tale about something that happened to us as a child that is the reason for why we are the way we are. And that is ok, it's been tough, and relaying that story has got you through some tricky times. Now its your chance to consider the possibility that the story no longer identifies you as a person. You are ready to move beyond that and towards the version of you who enjoys life and feels more fulfilled.

Not sure? See next page for Tips.

WRITE

What is the story that you tell yourself and others that's hindering your progress?

_____

_____

_____

_____

_____

_____

_____

_____

_____

_____

_____

_____

_____

_____

_____

_____

_____

_____

- You don't know where to start.
- Too many other people are doing it.
- You don't know what you want to do, that's the problem.
- You have too many other things to do.
- You don't have time.
- Your children/work/parents/siblings/housework takes up all your time.
- You're too tired.
- You have low self esteem, it's your parents' fault.
- You were bullied at school so you have no confidence in your abilities.
- You're too old to start now.
- Nothing inspires you.

The list is endless... but ultimately they are all just excuses for why we can't move forward with our lives, why we often feel stuck, and why we put the thing we'd actually much rather be doing to the bottom of the pile. Identifying the story, and therefore the unconscious pattern or program we are running, can help us move forward.

 Still Not Sure?

Let's do a little exercise that might help:
It's called 'Finding the Truth Behind the Tale'

Close your eyes, take a few slow, deep belly breaths. Focus on the story you tell others and yourself. Notice how it feels in the body – there'll be a sensation, perhaps a feeling of reassurance or calm even. That's because it's been your safety net for so long, but it's the story you hide behind to avoid the truth, and it's not serving your evolution. Notice where the sensation is located in the body. Breathe through the area and thank it for keeping you safe, but you've got it from here.

After a while, you will notice the sensation start to dissipate and subside.
Draw or write about it in your journal.

DRAW

If you could draw a representation of the story you tell yourself and others about why you're not doing what you most want to do, what would it look like?

STEP 4

>>>>>>>>>>

Inspiration Station

- What is something in your life that you can find joy in?
- What is it you love about doing it?
- Why does it bring you joy?

Joy comes from within not without. Finding joy in the little things is a great way to start cultivating the feeling of joy within yourself on a regular basis. Notice how it feels in your body when you feel joy, and focus on that. Find joy in another little thing and then another... until it becomes such a habit that you do it without thinking.

Not sure? See next page for Tips.

WRITE

Tell someone in the most excited and enthusiastic way you can about something ordinary you do often. Encourage someone through your words why they would enjoy it too.

_____

_____

_____

_____

_____

_____

_____

_____

_____

_____

_____

_____

_____

_____

_____

_____

_____

_____

_____

_____

Tips

- Hanging up the washing outside – how amazing it is that Mother Nature warms and dries the clothes for you, for free!
- Driving to work – listening to music, singing along at the top of your voice to your favourite tune, or listening to an inspiring podcast; a great time to reflect and enjoy time on your own.
- Walking the dog – how much joy do dogs feel at the simplest of things?
- Vacuuming – amazing invention that means you don't have to crawl around on your hands and knees with a brush!
- Food shopping – so much choice!
- Homework – knowledge is power.

Another trick to finding joy is to practise gratitude. Look around you and notice all the things in your life you are grateful for. If you had a beautiful meal and then had to wash-up afterwards, focus on the gratitude for the food rather than the mess that needed cleaning as a consequence. Then enjoy the way the soap bubbles in the sink shimmer with the colours of the rainbow.

Still Not Sure?

Let's do a little exercise that might help:
It's called 'Blowing up the Joy Bubble'

Take a few deep belly breaths. Feel yourself inside the body. Think of a time when you experienced something that made you feel great, something that you achieved or enjoyed immensely. Recall the memory in detail. Now notice how it feels in your body and focus on that feeling. Imagine it growing and filling your body, let it seep into every crevice until you are full of it. Then let it expand outwards until you are in the centre of a giant joy bubble. Enjoy the feeling for as long as you like.

Now it's about the feeling not the event. You can access that feeling whenever you want by doing this exercise regularly until you can conjure the feeling on command. The feeling of joy.

Practise feeling joy every day. Draw or write about it in your journal.

DRAW

What is something ordinary that you do often? Draw a picture expressing the joy you feel when doing it.

STEP 5

>>>>>>>>>>>>

Crossing Over

- What will it take to move forward?
- What are the steps towards a more fulfilling future?
- What needs to change?

Often it takes that one first step into a new reality to transform our lives. Then the next step, and the next... with complete trust that whatever is for our highest good will unfold in front of us. Check inside for what feels right for you, not what you think is right based on old beliefs and conditioning.

Not sure? See next page for Tips.

# WRITE

Compile a list of the things that you want to change in your life, and then alongside that, what you want to replace them with.

_____

_____

_____

_____

_____

_____

_____

_____

_____

_____

_____

_____

_____

_____

_____

_____

_____

_____

_____

_____

_____

_____

_____

_____

_____

_____

_____

Tips

- Recall that thing you put to the bottom of the pile; how could you move towards that rather than away from it?
- Where could you create more time during the day for what you enjoy?
- What is no longer serving you?
- Feel about the various aspects of your life – what feels good and what feels bad? Make two separate lists for each.
- What's one thing you could create in your life that's just for you?

Stepping into the unknown can be scary but also exciting – the possibilities are endless! What if you had complete creative freedom over how your life unfolds? (Hint: because you do). How would you show up differently? What changes would you make?

Still Not Sure?

Let's do a little exercise that might help: It's called 'Have It All'

Take a few deep belly breaths. Feel yourself inside the body. Start with Blowing up the Joy Bubble in the previous section. Now, in that elevated state of joy, picture the life you want to live. Focus on each detail whilst maintaining the good feeling. Believe that anything is possible in your new reality, and that you are the creator.

Now see how you feel about moving into the unknown, creating the life you want to live. Do you feel ready to change things up? Draw or write about it in your journal.

DRAW

Sketch a map or story board charting your next steps.
Or create a vision board using pictures and text
from old magazines.

STEP 6

>>>>>>>>>>>>>

Friend or Foe

- Who in your life right now has your back?
- And who might be holding you back?

People come and go in our lives but they are all here to teach us something or challenge us in some way. Thinking about those who serve your evolution and those who don't helps you realise your worth. What do you honour in a friend? How would you show up for someone else on their journey?

Not sure? See next page for Tips.

WRITE

How does the ideal companion compare to the people you already have in you life? Who would you leave behind and who would you take along on your journey and why?

_____
_____
_____
_____
_____
_____
_____
_____
_____
_____
_____
_____
_____
_____
_____
_____
_____
_____
_____
_____
_____
_____

Tips

- What qualities do you value in a friend or companion?
- Do you want someone who would be next to you when faced with a potential danger and fight alongside you? Or someone who would use you as a human shield?
- Do you like those who challenge you, or obey your every word?
- Who makes you want to be a better person?
- Who is a true reflection of you – the good and bad?
- Who will love you no matter what?

Someone who you'd want with you should challenge and support you in equal measure. People who put you down and project their lack of self-worth are not serving you. Consider that those in your immediate environment can also reflect aspects of you; therefore changing your outlook and how you feel about yourself internally will also effect change externally. Love yourself, be kind to yourself, be generous and loving to others, and they will reflect those things back to you.

Still Not Sure?

Let's do a little exercise that might help: It's called **'Finding Love on the Inside'**

Take a few deep belly breaths. Feel yourself inside the body. Think of someone you love; a person or even a pet. Fill your heart with the love you feel for them. Let it fill your body. Breathe it into every part of your being until you are filled with love. Notice how it feels. Revel in it.

This love comes from within, it is not sent from the person or pet that you are visualising right now, it's all coming from you. You can conjure this feeling of love whenever you want, in any situation, by practising this technique and remembering how it feels in your body. The more time you spend cultivating this feeling, the more easily you will access it and the more people who reflect that love will be drawn to you. Could these be the companions and friends that you want on your journey?

Now see how you feel about friends and foe. Do you feel ready to choose who's coming along on your journey? Draw or write about it in your journal.

DRAW

Who is the ideal companion on your journey into the unknown world: this next phase of your life? It can be someone you already know, or someone you would like to attract into your life.

STEP 7

The Challenge

- What do you still have to face?
- What past events still have a hold over you?
- What or who presents the biggest challenge in your life right now?

A possible way to identify this nemesis is to think about what patterns we repeat in our lives. What is it that keeps reoccurring? What are you most afraid of? Often it takes the form of self-doubt, lack of self-worth and confidence in your abilities. The initial seed of doubt was possibly planted by a life circumstance but really it's all coming from within us; our own self-chatter, self criticism.

Not sure? See next page for Tips.

WRITE

Describe the challenge or nemesis in detail. Write a conversation between you both. Ask it what it's here to show you. What does it reply?

_____
_____
_____
_____
_____
_____
_____
_____
_____
_____
_____
_____
_____
_____
_____
_____
_____
_____
_____
_____
_____
_____

Tips

- Are there repeating patterns in your life – bad business decisions, unsupportive relationships, people being unkind, rejection...?
- Is your self-esteem low?
- Does every relationship you have end in betrayal?
- Do you get so close to what you want and then it all falls apart at the last minute?
- No matter how hard you try, manifestation doesn't work for you.
- If you do the thing you want to do, people will judge you.
- Perhaps it's a feeling, a block that appears every time you think about doing the thing.
- Perhaps you've tried many times and failed.
- Perhaps you don't even know what it is you want to do.

Often the thing in our way is ourselves, and it's only because of our perception of the outside world that we blame something 'out there'. But in reality it's all coming from within us. If 'out there' is merely a reflection of 'in here' (because it is), then how do we alter our internal reality to make a positive change in our lives? It's all about self-belief and knowing that we create our own reality every day in everything we do. Yes, we are that powerful. So what is stopping you?

Still Not Sure?

Let's do a little exercise that might help:
It's called  'Show Me Yours and I'll Show You Mine'

Take a few deep belly breaths. Feel yourself inside the body. When you think about the thing you most want to do, what happens in your body? Get into the habit of constantly checking in with how you feel. Notice where in the body you feel a charge – a twist in your gut, a closing of your throat, a pain in your heart. What does it feel like? How does it look? Notice the colour, consistency, is it moving or still? Is there a sound associated with it? Notice everything about it. Now ask it what it wants – this is your nemesis.

Now see how you feel about your biggest challenge. Do you feel ready to face it? Draw or write about it in your journal.

DRAW

What does the thing that is the biggest challenge to you look like? This is your nemesis. Give it colour and shape, really feel into the emotions it brings up.

STEP 8

>>>>>>>>>>>>>

Face Off

- Are you ready to stand your ground and face your fears?
- Look it in the eye and don't be afraid.
- Say thank you for what it's teaching you.

Despite how bad it can make you feel, it's not there to hurt you, only show you a part of yourself that you've closed off, locked away; where the energy is unable to flow. It just wants your attention so you can release it and let it go. It's holding you back from being your true, authentic self. Don't let it control your life anymore!

Not sure? See next page for Tips.

WRITE

A thankyou letter to your nemesis. You appreciate all it's shown you about yourself, but it's no longer serving you and your highest good.

_____

_____

_____

_____

_____

_____

_____

_____

_____

_____

_____

_____

_____

_____

_____

_____

_____

_____

_____

_____

_____

Tips

- The thing you are most afraid to face is the thing that is there to teach you the greatest lesson.
- It has been languishing in the dark depths for too long, it needs to be brought up to the light.
- It can't hurt you if you face it, only if you continue to ignore it.
- Feel it, love it, forgive it, thank it.

Facing your challenge is the only way to move past it. It will keep rearing its ugly head and knocking on your door until you start paying attention. You can't outrun it forever. The longer you ignore it, the more likely it will be that it will grow into something even more terrifying; like pain in your body or mental illness. It will keep trying to get your attention until you notice it. All it wants is love.

Still Not Sure?

Let's do a little exercise that might help: It's called 'Love Your Enemy'

Take a few deep belly breaths. Feel yourself inside the body. Do the Show Me Yours and I'll Show You Mine exercise in the previous section. When you are face to face with your nemesis in whatever form that takes for you, love it, hug it, thank it. It will writhe around and try to get away, don't let it. It's forgotten what love feels like; remind it. Stay with it. Breathe. Cry if you want to, laugh. Let the emotions flow. Then release it, watch it dissipate and fall away as if it was never there. Love into the parts of yourself that are left.

Now you have faced your biggest challenge and let it go. Draw or write about it in your journal.

DRAW

If a confrontation occurred between you and your greatest challenge, how would it play out? Perhaps draw a comic strip showing the process.

STEP 9

>>>>>>>>>>>>

Telling a New Story

- How has facing this challenge served you?
- What have you learned about yourself?

In the story you have been telling people about why you can't do the thing you most want to do, you have been the victim; life has been happening to you. Rewriting it from a positive perspective, showing how it has brought you to this place of realisation, transforms you from the victim to the hero – the creator of your own reality. This is your chance to move into your greatness.

Not sure? See next page for Tips.

WRITE

Rewrite your story in a positive way. Become the hero rather than the victim of your own life.

_____

_____

_____

_____

_____

_____

_____

_____

_____

_____

_____

_____

_____

_____

_____

_____

_____

_____

_____

_____

Tips

- Perhaps you were shouted at as a child and never listened to so you find it hard to speak your truth for fear of reprimand. How has that served you? What has it made you realise about yourself? Could it be that you are worthy of being heard and it's time to realise that?

- Maybe you were bullied at school and that's why you seek approval from others all the time and never actually finish anything you start. How has that served you? What has it made you realise about yourself? Could it be that you don't need others' approval after all?

- It could be that you have a fear of crowds because all those people make you feel anxious. How has that served you? What has it made you realise about yourself? Perhaps that the anxiety you feel is the creative essence in you stirring, desperate to be seen and be a part of that crowd.

Life happens for you not against you. Every apparent hardship is a lesson on your journey to self-actualisation. Each challenge overcome is up-levelling you to a new, enlightened state. See the difficult times as an opportunity to move beyond what you have come to expect as normal. This is your chance to become extraordinary!

Still Not Sure?

Let's do a little exercise that might help: It's called 'Embody the YES!' a few deep belly breaths. Feel yourself inside. Now focus on the word YES. Notice how the word feels in your body. Imagine doing the thing you most want to do, imagine how it would feel in your body; the sense of achievement, the joy, the empowerment of creating the thing you want the most. Now repeat YES over and over. And so it is.

You are the creator of your own reality, not at the mercy of it. Draw or write about it in your journal.

DRAW

How has the story you have been telling people actually been in your favour? You could draw yourself transforming from ordinary person to super hero.

STEP 10

>>>>>>>>>>>

Making Space

● In order to embrace the new, you must release the old.
● What is still to be released and let go of?

The first steps to becoming this new version of yourself is to decide what to keep and what to discard. It's time for a spring clean! Declutter your world to make space for the new things. Take a look in all the boxes that you have buried deep in the basement of your being that still contain things from your past. Why are you keeping them? Do they serve a purpose or just remind you of your unworthiness? Only keep what makes you feel good – ditch the rest (don't forget to say thank you for the lessons).

Not sure? See next page for Tips.

WRITE

What boxes are still left to unpack in the basement of your being? List what to keep and what to discard.

_____

_____

_____

_____

_____

_____

_____

_____

_____

_____

_____

_____

_____

_____

_____

_____

_____

_____

_____

_____

Tips

- What or who from your past does not serve your future?
- When you arrive home from this journey you've been on, as the new version of yourself, how will you feel about your old life and the things in it? What will you want to keep and what would you rather discard?
- This is not just an external process, it's internal too. Look inside for those underlying and repeating patterns.
- Clearing out the old makes room for the new, it's a necessary process on the journey of up-levelling to a new version self.

It may sound ruthless and drastic to make such changes, but there will be things in your life that perhaps you hadn't realised (or maybe you had!) weren't benefitting you and your evolution. And these things can be internal or external. The boxes are symbolic of the parts of you internally that are no longer serving you (negative thought patterns, hidden fears, suppressed emotions), as well as the external stuff in your garage or attic. Take time to look deeply into these things and consider what should stay and what should go.

Still Not Sure?

Let's do a little exercise that might help: It's called 'Body Scan for the Truth'

Take a few deep belly breaths. Feel yourself inside the body. Now think of something you're unclear about whether it's benefitting you, helping you move forward – it can be a person, situation, or circumstance. Notice how it feels in the body when you think of that thing. Where do you feel a reaction – a charge, a knot, a twist? Or does it make you feel joyful and elated? Notice the feeling and whether it's something you want to feel whenever you are with that person or in that situation. You get to choose.

Feel inside for the truth and you will know what to do. Now draw or write about it in your journal.

DRAW

A representation of what you are letting go of – perhaps
a fire burning up all the things that are no longer
serving you.

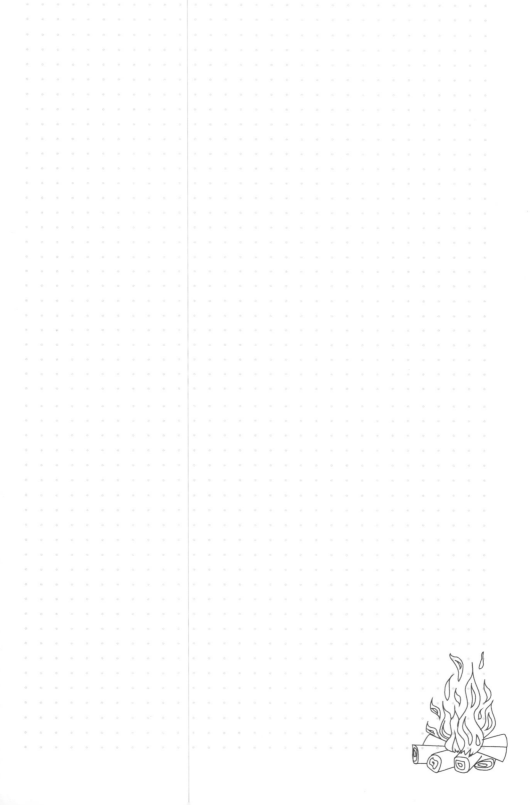

STEP 11

The Altered Self

- What are you like now?
- How do you now present out into the world?
- What changes will people notice about you?

How will you operate out in the world differently from how you did before? The changes in you will be apparent to others – they will be subtle but noticeable – how you might now react differently to a situation that would usually have had your shields up, sword drawn. Remember, your exterior environment mirrors your interior environment. Enter a room feeling joyful and smiling, that is where people will meet you. Be defensive and ready for a fight, so they will meet you on the battle field.

 *Not sure?* See next page for Tips.

WRITE

Describe yourself and how you will action out in the world as this new version.

_____
_____
_____
_____
_____
_____
_____
_____
_____
_____
_____
_____
_____
_____
_____
_____
_____
_____
_____
_____
_____
_____
_____

Tips

- Now that you have made space by clearing out what is not working in your favour, what is left?
- How are you going to react differently to situations?
- How do you feel different?
- What does this new version look like to you and others?
- Perhaps you will change the way you talk about things — words are spells after all, so use words that speak to the kind of person you want to be and the life you want to create.

You are in control of two things in your life — how you feel and how you operate out in the world. No one can choose those things for you. Every feeling, every reaction that is a result of those feelings, is a choice that you can make. So how will you respond? How will you engage? What do you want to receive from others? Lead by example. Give to others and you will receive. Love yourself and you will receive love. Be grateful every day and your bounties will grow exponentially.

Still Not Sure?

Let's do a little exercise that might help:
It's called 'Feel the Feeling you Want to Feel'

Take a few deep belly breaths. Feel yourself inside the body. Imagine a situation in which you would normally be defensive. Notice how your body contracts as if an armour has been built around you and trapped you inside. Breathe into your heart space and feel it opening and expanding out through the armour and towards the person or situation you are imagining. Let the love dissolve the armour, let it fall away. You are now surrounded by a field of love. That is the only armour you need.

This is the new version of you in its purest form. Now draw or write about it in your journal.

DRAW

What does the new you look like?

STEP 12
>>>>>>>>>>>>>

A New World

- What does this new world look like?
- You have a blank canvas, start creating from your heart.
- What do you desire?

Now you have created a new version of yourself, you are ready to create the new world you want to live in. What does it look like? You have a blank canvas; a seed from which to grow whatever you desire. Anything is possible. Go inside and feel your way to a new reality that makes your heart sing. Believe you can create whatever you want, because you can. Everything in the past has been dissolved, it no longer exists unless you want it to.

Not sure? See next page for Tips.

WRITE

A new story, your life starts here.

_____
_____
_____
_____
_____
_____
_____
_____
_____
_____
_____
_____
_____
_____
_____
_____
_____
_____
_____
_____
_____
_____
_____
_____

Tips

- You have been on an epic journey of self-discovery, what have you learned?

- What did you discover about the person you want to be and the life you want to lead?

- Who and what inspires you to be a better version of yourself?

- What brings you joy and fulfilment? Feel inside for the answers.

- This is not about what you should do, this about what you desire. Dismantle the old belief systems and conformities, they no longer apply. This is your life to do with what you will. Take back control.

- Allow your greatness to be true!

This is your chance to build a new world with everything in it reflecting the truth of who you are. Let the child within have his/her voice back. Allow playfulness, joy, love, creation, wisdom, gratitude, and kindness to be the truth of you. There is nothing you are not. It's time to remember why you came and what you chose to create while you were here. It's not meant to be a life of pain and hardship, it's a playground – so play!

Still Not Sure?

Let's do a little exercise that might help:
It's called  'Remembering the Child Within'

Take a few deep belly breaths. Feel yourself inside the body. Imagine walking into a meadow with long grass that tickles your legs, the warm sun on your skin. See a child playing in the meadow; that is you. Walk up to the child and ask if you can play. Feel the purity and joy in their response as they say YES! Ask them what makes them happy, what they love to do. What were their hopes and dreams for their life? What did they want to be? Allow that one to have a say in your new world.

You can now create this life in collaboration with the child within you. Draw or write about it in your journal.

DRAW

The life you desire.

NOTES

Thoughts, Inspiration, Ideas...